What's My Style?

I love creating elaborate patterns packed with detail so I can do lots of intricate coloring. I try to use as many colors as possible. Then, I layer on lots of fun details. Here are some more examples of my work.

With my love of detail and coloring, I can easily fill up entire pages of journals like these!

Tips and Techniques

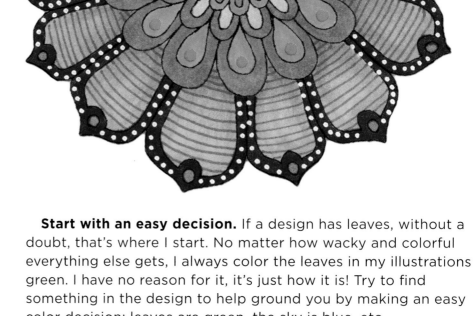

WHERE TO START

You might find putting color on a fresh page stressful. It's ok! Here are a few tricks I use to get the ink flowing.

Do you like warm colors?

How about cool colors?

Maybe you like warm and cool colors together!

Start with an easy decision. If a design has leaves, without a doubt, that's where I start. No matter how wacky and colorful everything else gets, I always color the leaves in my illustrations green. I have no reason for it, it's just how it is! Try to find something in the design to help ground you by making an easy color decision: leaves are green, the sky is blue, etc.

Get inspired. Take a good look at everything in the illustration. You chose to color it for a reason. One little piece that you love will jump out and say, "Color me! Use red, please!" Or maybe it will say blue, or pink, or green. Just relax—it will let you know.

Follow your instincts. What colors do you love? Are you a big fan of purple? Or maybe yellow is your favorite. If you love it, use it!

Just go for it. Close your eyes, pick up a color, point to a spot on the illustration, and start! Sometimes starting is the hardest part, but it's the fastest way to finish!

HELPFUL HINTS

There is no right or wrong. All colors work together, so don't be scared to mix it up. The results can be surprising!

Try it. Test your chosen colors on scrap paper before you start coloring your design. You can also test blending techniques and how to use different shapes and patterns for detail work—you can see how different media will blend with or show up on top of your chosen colors. I even use the paper to clean my markers or pens if necessary.

Make a color chart. A color chart is like a test paper for every single color you have! It provides a more accurate way to choose colors than selecting them based on the color of the marker's cap. To make a color chart, color a swatch with each marker, colored pencil, gel pen, etc. Label each swatch with the name or number of the marker so you can easily find it later.

Keep going. Even if you think you've ruined a piece, work through it. I go through the same cycle with my coloring: I love a piece at the beginning, and by the halfway point I nearly always dislike it. Sometimes by the end I love it again, and sometimes I don't, and that's ok. It's important to remember that you're coloring for you—no one else. If you really don't like a piece at the end, stash it away and remember that you learned something. You know what not to do next time. My studio drawers are full of everything from duds to masterpieces!

Be patient. Let markers, gel pens, and paints dry thoroughly between each layer. There's nothing worse than smudging a cluster of freshly inked dots across the page with your hand. Just give them a minute to dry and you can move on to the next layer.

Use caution. Juicy/inky markers can "spit" when you uncap them. Open them away from your art piece.

Work from light to dark. It's much easier to make something darker gradually than to lighten it.

Shade with gray. A mid-tone lavender-gray marker is perfect for adding shadows to your artwork, giving it depth and making it pop right off the page!

Try blending fluid. If you like working with alcohol-based markers, a refillable bottle of blending fluid or a blending pen is a great investment. Aside from enabling you to easily blend colors together, it can help clean up unwanted splatters or mistakes—it may not take some colors away completely, but it will certainly lighten them. I use it to clean the body of my markers as I'm constantly smudging them with inky fingers. When a marker is running out of ink, I find adding a few drops of blending fluid to the ink barrel will make it last a bit longer.

LAYERING AND BLENDING

I love layering and blending colors. It's a great way to create shading and give your finished piece lots of depth and dimension. The trick is to work from the lightest color to the darkest and then go over everything again with the lightest shade to keep the color smooth and bring all the layers together.

1 Apply a base layer with the lightest color.

2 Add the middle color, using it to create shading.

3 Smooth out the color by going over everything with the lightest color.

4 Add the darkest color, giving your shading even more depth. Use the middle color to go over the same area you colored in Step 2.

5 Go over everything with the lightest color as you did in Step 3.

PATTERNING AND DETAILS

Layering and blending will give your coloring depth and dimension. Adding patterning and details will really bring it to life. If you're not convinced, try adding a few details to one of your colored pieces with a white gel pen—that baby will make magic happen! Have fun adding all of the dots, doodles, and swirls you can imagine.

1 Once you've finished your coloring, blending, and layering, go back and add simple patterning like lines or dots. You can add your patterns in black or color. For this leaf, I used two different shades of green pen.

2 Now it's time to add some fun details using paint pens or gel pens. Here, I used white, yellow, and more green.

This design really pops with lots of patterning and little details.

Coloring Supplies

I'm always asked about the mediums I use to color my illustrations. The answer would be really long if I listed every single thing, so here are a few of my favorites. Keep in mind, these are *my* favorites. When you color, you should use YOUR favorites!

Alcohol-based markers. I have many, and a variety of brands. My favorites have a brush nib—it's so versatile. A brush nib is perfect for tiny, tight corners, but also able to cover a large, open space easily. I find I rarely get streaking, and if I do, it's usually because the ink is running low!

Fine-tip pens. Just like with markers, I have lots of different pens. I use them for my layers of detail work and for the itsy bitsy spots my markers can't get into.

Paint pens. These are wonderful! Because the ink is usually opaque, they stand out really well against a dark base color. I use extra fine point pens for their precision. Some paint pens are water based, so I can use a brush to blend the colors and create a cool watercolor effect.

Gel pens. I have a few, but I usually stick to white and neon colors that will stand out on top of dark base colors or other mediums.

Hello Angel #1142, Color by Darla Tjelmeland

Hello Angel #1138, Color by Darla Tjelmeland

Hello Angel #1156, Color by Darla Tjelmeland

Hello Angel #1152, Color by Darla Tjelmeland

Hello Angel #1150, Color by Darla Tjelmeland

Hello Angel #1145, Color by Hello Angel

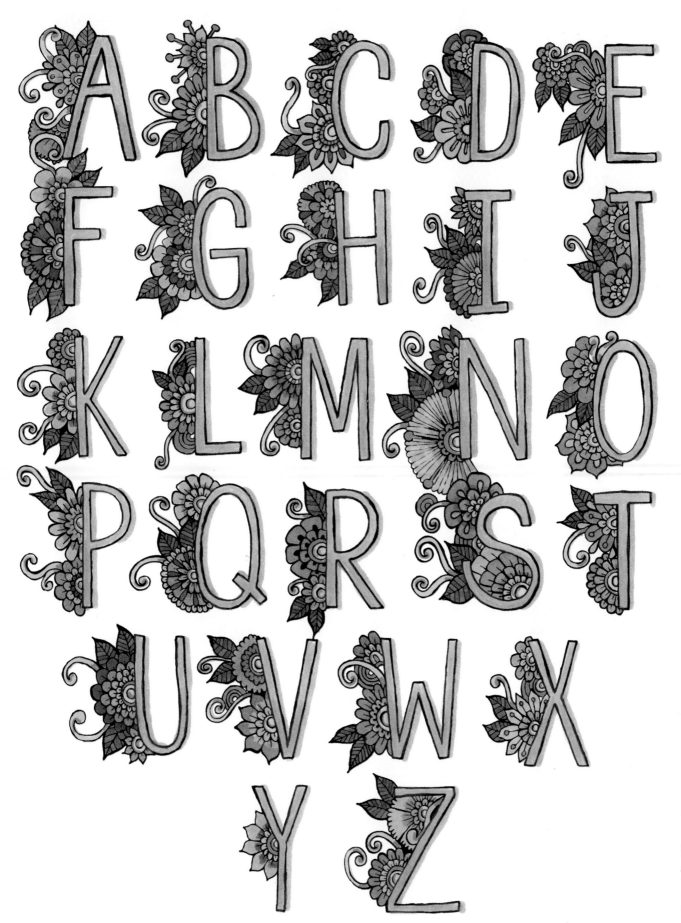

Hello Angel #1136, Color by Darla Tjelmeland

Hello Angel #1157, Color by Darla Tjelmeland

As Easy As A, B, C!

The next few pages are filled with beautiful alphabet motifs featuring letters from designs throughout the book. Have fun coloring each motif, or color a few letters that are special to you, like your initials. Each page is perforated, so you easily remove a page and cut out letters to create your own work of art. After the alphabets, you'll find pages packed with positive words and sayings to brighten up your day and inspire you. Now get coloring! It's as easy as A, B, C!

It always seems impossible until it's done.

—UNKNOWN

Sometimes what you're most afraid of doing is
the very thing that will set you free.

—Unknown

Every morning we are born again.
What we do today is what matters most.

—UNKNOWN

Every day may not be good, but there
is something good in every day.

—UNKNOWN

A person who never made a mistake
never tried anything new.

—UNKNOWN

Being challenged in life is inevitable.
Being defeated is optional.

—ROGER CRAWFORD

It's never too late to be what you might have been.

—Unknown

_____
_____
_____
_____
_____
_____
_____
_____
_____

If plan A doesn't work,
the alphabet has 25 more letters.

—UNKNOWN

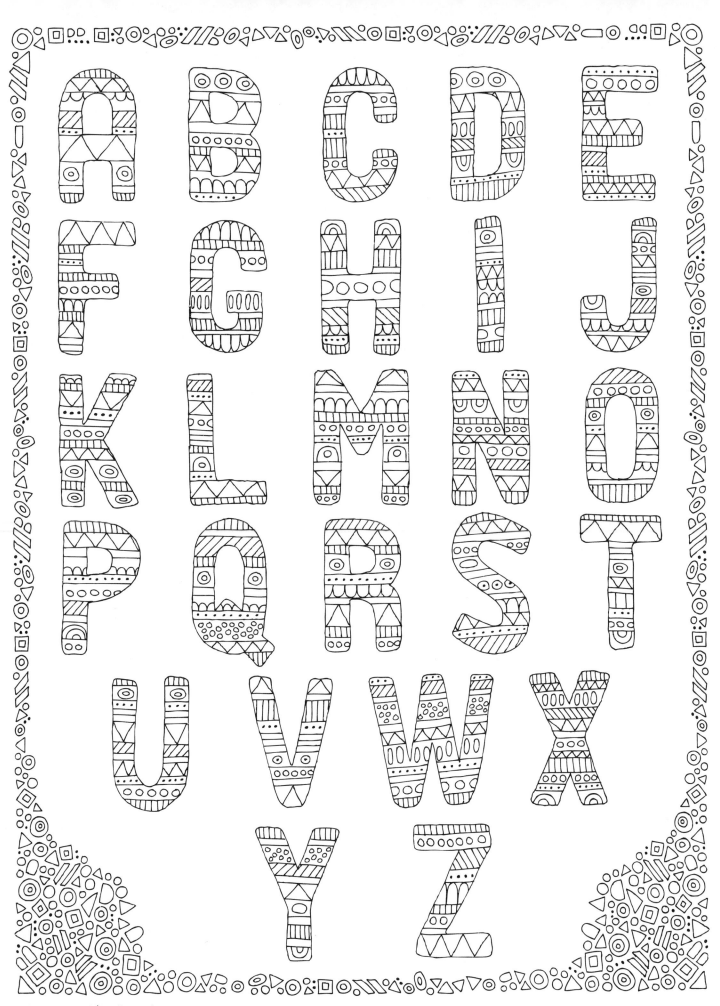

Think big thoughts but relish small pleasures.

—H. JACKSON BROWN, JR.

Your life is your message to the world.
Make sure it's inspiring.

—UNKNOWN

There is sunshine in my soul today.

—UNKNOWN

Those who dare to fail miserably
can achieve greatly.

—JOHN F. KENNEDY

I have found that if you love life,
life will love you back.

—Arthur Rubinstein

The moments of happiness we enjoy take us by surprise. It is not that we seize them, but that they seize us.

—ASHLEY MONTAGU

Life is one grand, sweet song,
so start the music.

—UNKNOWN

Moon dust in your lungs, stars in your eyes,
you are a child of the cosmos,
a ruler of the skies.

—Unknown

It's a good day to have a good day.

—UNKNOWN

Know who you are, and be it.
Know what you want, and go out and get it!

—CARROLL BRYANT

You can't use up creativity. The more you use,
the more you have.

—MAYA ANGELOU

_____
_____
_____
_____
_____
_____
_____
_____
_____

When we have each other, we have everything.

—UNKNOWN

Life is tough, my darling, but so are you.

—Unknown

There are so many beautiful
reasons to be happy.

—UNKNOWN

Be brave enough to live life creatively.

—ALAN ALDA

_____
_____
_____
_____
_____
_____
_____
_____
_____
_____

Life is a blank canvas, and you need to throw all the paint on it you can.

—Danny Kaye

I am my own work of art.

—MADONNA

An awake heart is like a sky that pours light.

—HᾱFEZ

And so the adventure begins.

—UNKNOWN

Be YOU tiful

Be so happy that when others look at you,
they become happy too.

—UNKNOWN

I wandered everywhere, through cities and countries wide. And everywhere I went, the world was on my side.

—ROMAN PAYNE

Believe you can and you're halfway there.

—THEODORE ROOSEVELT

_____
_____
_____
_____
_____
_____
_____
_____
_____

Don't worry about failures, worry about the chances you miss when you don't even try.

—JACK CANFIELD

When life puts you in tough situations,
don't say, "Why me." Say, "Try me."

—UNKNOWN